THE UNOFFICIAL
Chappell Roan
Join the Pink Pony Club in a KALEIDOSCOPE of Color
COLORING BOOK
illustrated by
Taylor Barron
mudpuppy
I0606381

Midwest Princess

Celebrate the rise of America's favorite prom queen. Chappell Roan—born Kayleigh Rose Amstutz—nods to her Missouri roots with the title of her debut album, *The Rise and Fall of a Midwest Princess.* Even her stage name is filled with meaning: it's a tribute to her late grandfather, Dennis K. Chappell, who loved the classic song "Strawberry Roan." From her name to her music, every choice Chappell makes is deliberate and deeply personal.

PROM QUEEN

Armor Up

Bold, brash, and battle-ready—Chappell isn't just playing dress-up. When she wore a Joan of Arc–style suit of armor during a fiery performance of "Good Luck, Babe!" at the Video Music Awards, she showed off her fierce independence. That same night, she accepted the award for "Best New Artist."

Regal Reverie

Chappell grew up feeling like she had to shrink herself. Now, she does the opposite. At a 2024 Lollapalooza performance, she appeared in full Marie Antoinette glam—a corseted gown, towering wig, and powdered face—embracing excess and fantasy as forms of freedom. The look, inspired by the queen who was seen as "too much," reflects Chappell's journey from repression to unapologetic self-expression.

Cheerleader Anthem

As a high schooler, Chappell fantasized about being a cheerleader. Her local cheer team was "just so cool and hot," but she never tried out because she feared she didn't belong. Two weeks before her debut headlining tour, Chappell tapped into her self-confidence and reimagined her childhood dream by releasing "HOT TO GO!" a sassy and silly cheer hit with its own accompanying routine that *Cosmopolitan* dubbed the best song of 2024.

CHAPPELL
U

Pink Pony Club

After a bold move from the Midwest to the West Coast, one of Chappell's first stops was The Abbey in West Hollywood. Filled with love, pride, and acceptance, this nightclub made Chappell feel for the first time that she could truly be herself. As she watched the go-go dancers sparkle on stage, inspiration struck and Chappell wrote the now-iconic "Pink Pony Club" about the exhilarating feeling of liberation.

Definition of Dedication

Grab your closest dictionary and you're certain to see Chappell's picture next to the definition of "dedication." Her commitment to her art is admirable: after being dropped by Atlantic Records in 2020, she continued to develop her craft. Chappell balanced her love for music with her need to support herself, working as a nanny, a production assistant, and a donut shop employee while also working as an independent artist for three years before signing with Island Records in 2023.

DONUTS
1 DONUT
1/2 DOZEN
1 DOZEN
6 DONUT HOLES
12 DONUT HOLES
COFFEE
ESPRESSO
LATTE

Love Wins

"Thank God for you," Chappell penned in a 2023 love letter to her supporters for Billboard. Chappell credits her devoted, loyal fans for saving her and allowing her to truly be herself. In turn, Chappell has become a champion for individuality and embracing people's differences, creating a safe space for fans to discover who they really are.

LOVE
PRIDE

Damsel, Not in Distress

Chappell had a triumphant return to the road in the fall of 2025, when she set off on a mini headlining tour called Visions of Damsels & Other Dangerous Things. She performed hits from *Midwest Princess* and her three newer singles at pop-up shows in New York City, Los Angeles, and Kansas City. For each ticket sold, Chappell donated a dollar to youth-based charities, proving herself to be a loving and compassionate queen of her kingdom.

SOUR Sisters

Pop princesses stick together! Chappell has an iconic friendship with fellow popstar Olivia Rodrigo thanks to their shared producer, Dan Nigro. In 2022 and 2024, Chappell opened both of Olivia's headlining tours, even showing up at a GUTS show to perform "HOT TO GO!" with Liv. If you listen closely, you may be able to hear Chappell's backing vocals on Olivia's songs "lacy," "Can't Catch Me Now," and "get him back!"

Hot to go

She's Got A Way

She's not just another girl on the subway, Chappell Roan is an undeniable global superstar. When she debuted "The Subway" at the Governors Ball Musical Festival in 2024, fans began clamoring for the studio version to be released. They waited over a year for it to happen. Critics showered the song with praise while the hit climbed the charts all over the world.

M
EXIT

Like and Subscribe

Chappell started her music career like so many Millennial and Gen Z superstars before her: on YouTube. As a teenager, she posted covers and original songs that eventually attracted the attention of Atlantic Records. Fellow YouTuber turned pop artist Troye Sivan was one of Chappell's first fans, tweeting in 2014, "LETS BLOW KAYLEIGH UP BC I HAVENT HEARD A VOICE LIKE THIS SINCE ADELE, NO EXAGGERATION."

Grammy Goddess

Avid watchers of the Grammy Awards know the Big Four: Best New Artist, Song of the Year, Record of the Year, and Album of the Year. At the 67th Grammys, Chappell scored nominations for all of these categories and won her first Grammy for Best New Artist. In classic Chappell fashion, her style paid tribute to artists who came before her. She wore a gown that nodded to the famous Edgar Degas painting, *The Ballerinas*.

Siren Song

Chappell takes playing mermaids very seriously. In the music video for "Casual," a yearning ballad about an ill-fated relationship, her character falls in love with a sparkling scale-covered siren. When talking to *Teen Vogue* about the colorful under-the-sea themed music video, she compared it to the mermaid movie, *Aquamarine*.

Christmas Carols

'Twas the night before Christmas, and all through the house, everyone was streaming Chappell Roan and Sabrina Carpenter's duet of "Last Christmas." Chappell was one of the highly-anticipated guest performers on "A Nonsense Christmas with Sabrina Carpenter," where she and Sabrina stunned in velvet dresses and big fur coats. Their duet was a true present to fans, many of whom are hoping another collaboration is in the future.

She Gets The Job Done

Construction worker, plumber, dentist, lawyer, private eye—Chappell can do it all. Or, at least, she can release cute posters and billboards of herself doing it all while promoting her 2025 single, "The Giver." First performed on *Saturday Night Live*, this upbeat country hit mixes Chappell's midwest roots with her love for women. When it comes to romance, Chappell sings, women can always get the job done.

TION
CAUTIO
CAUTION
CAUTION
AUTION

Celebrating Her Inner Child

When it comes to her music career, Chappell isn't in it for the fame and fortune. Instead, as she explained to fans on Instagram: "I chose this career path because I love music and art and honoring my inner child." At the end of the day, she's truly making art for the little midwestern girl she once was who didn't know that the world had so much to offer her.

Chappell Roan

Live from New York

Chappell may also be the queen of manifestation. Way back in 2011, she posted on Facebook, "I am determined to be on *SNL*." Flash forward thirteen years later, and Chappell is draped in beads and feathers on the *Saturday Night Live* stage, singing "Pink Pony Club" to a crowd of adoring fans. This dream come true was one of many for Chappell, and it certainly won't be her last!

ALL ARE WELCOME

Your Favorite Artist's Favorite Artist

There would be no Chappell Roan if it weren't for drag queens. Chappell credits drag artists for inspiring her bold aesthetics and artistry, even showcasing local drag queens as openers for her shows. When she met one of her drag idols, Sasha Colby, it was mutual love at first sight. Sasha dubbed Chappell her "drag daughter" and welcomed her into the House of Colby.

An Absolute Gem

Chappell is a big star with an even bigger heart. Now that she's the talk of the music industry, she's using her platform for good. Chappell has been vocal when it comes to supporting the rights and feelings of others. She also puts her money where her mouth is, raising funds for charities like For The Gworls, Mercy-USA, and The Glo Center.

Serving Looks

Beads? Check. Feathers? Check. Sequins? Check. Chappell Roan's style is a key part of her identity, making so many of her iconic looks on her own. "If a five-year-old could draw a popstar, it would be me," she joked with *Rolling Stone*, dubbing herself "a thrift-store popstar" and a "DIY queen." From hot gluing Gushers onto her shirt to working with stylists to craft imaginative hits, no one can ever guess what Chappell will wear next.

VINTAGE

Happy Camper

Chappell credits summer camp for "literally changing [her] life." At The Interlochen Center for the Arts in Michigan, Chappell was surrounded by kids from all over whom she deemed inspiring, exposing her to a creative world she had never been part of before. That summer, she wrote "Die Young," a song that caught the attention of record labels.

Madame Maestro

Everyone knows Chappell as a rising singer-songwriter turned popstar phenomenon, but she's also a talented musician. She's been playing the piano since she was a kid and began taking lessons at twelve, which helped her refine her natural musical skills. It's thanks to her love for and commitment to playing piano that we have the iconic opening riff of "Pink Pony Club."

Star Power

After years of chasing her dream of singing, Chappell finally made it big when *The Rise and Fall of Midwest Princess* blew up, topping the charts, winning critical praise, and bringing in millions of fans. And that was just her first album! This is just the beginning for Chappell Roan. Her future is bright and the whole world cannot wait to see what she does next.

www.mudpuppy.com • f @mudpuppykids
70 West 36th Street
New York, NY 10018

Editorial by Kate Rispoli
Illustrations by Taylor Barron

ISBN: 978-0-7353-8859-8

First Edition: 2026
Designed and printed in the United States of America.
10 9 8 7 6 5 4 3 2 1